TEDDY BEARS

A CELEBRATION

TEDDY BEARS

A CELEBRATION

Mary Hillier

FLIRTATION.

TEDDY

IT'S SO SIMPLE.

EBURY PRESS

LONDON

Published by Ebury Press
National Magazine House
72 Broadwick Street
London W1V 2BP

First impression 1985

ISBN: 0-85223-408-2

Created, designed and produced by Black Pig Editions Ltd
(Justin Knowles Publishing Group), P.O. Box 99,
Exeter, Devon, England.

Editors: Christopher Pick and Charlotte Parry-Crooke
Design: Tim Harvey and Roger Huggett
Production: Nick Facer

Typeset by P & M Typesetting Ltd, Exeter, England
Printed and bound in Italy by New Interlitho SPA, Milan

Publisher's Note

Of all toys, the Teddy Bear sustains a universal appeal. Cherished by boys and girls alike the world over, the charismatic Teddy is unique. We would like to thank everyone who contributed to this celebration, especially Pam Hebbs, Joan Dunk, Jennifer Bulbeck and Dorothy Kavanagh, all of whom are dedicated collectors. Special thanks go to Mary Hillier, whose informative text adds further dimension to this most lovable character, the Teddy Bear.

Contents

A row of Teddy bears sitting in a toyshop,
all one size, all one price. Yet how different
each is from the next. Some look gay, some look sad.
Some look stand-offish, some look lovable.
And one in particular… that one over there…
has a specially endearing expression.
Yes, that is the one we would like, please.

The Enchanted Places
by Christopher Milne, 1974

An early example of a Teddy made by the German firm of Steiff, one of the two contenders for the title of the inventor of the toy bear. The other was Morris Michtom of the American Ideal Toy Corporation. This large Steiff Teddy, made in 1908, has exceptionally long arms and huge feet.

HONEY

Will the First Teddy Bear Please Stand Up?

Who can imagine a world without Teddy Bears? In the present climate of their cult status it is difficult for collectors to believe that there was ever a time before they existed. But their origin is relatively modern and dates from no earlier than the start of the 20th century.

An interesting mythology has developed around their beginnings. In the game of 'Will the First Teddy Bear Please Stand Up?' we have to consider various contestants. There is, for instance, the story that Edward VII was especially fond of a little Australian Koala Bear at the London Zoo, which was called Teddy Bear in his honour. (In fact the Koala is not a bear at all but a marsupial.) This would explain why a number of early toy bears were called 'Edward'. Perhaps it also promoted the apocryphal tale that one of the King's lady friends remarked that 'she liked her Teddy bare'!

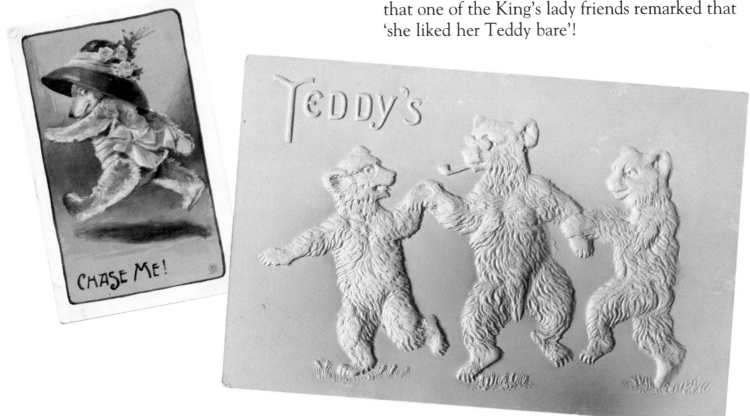

CHASE ME!

TEDDY'S

DRAWING
THE LINE
IN MISSISSIPPI

B————— 1902

Teddy's sporting tips

Left: Clifford Berryman's famous cartoon of President 'Teddy' Roosevelt and the bear cub he refused to kill. First published in 1902 in the *Washington Star*, 'Drawing the line in Mississippi' had a *double entendre*, since Roosevelt was on a mission to settle a border line dispute. It was also probably the inspiration for the first American Teddy Bear. The powerful appeal of Berryman's cartoon was responsible for many other Teddy depictions along the same lines, such as the example shown above.

Opposite: Morris Michtom, the self-proclaimed American inventor of the first Teddy Bear. The German toy manufacturer Steiff challenged such claims as bear-faced impertinence.

In the American Corner…

At the beginning of the century there was another famous Teddy: Theodore Roosevelt, who became President of the USA on the assassination of William McKinley in 1901. We can assume that the name was adopted as a result of an intriguing incident publicized in the *Washington Star* in 1902. The President, an enthusiastic hunter, had attended a hunt for Grizzly bear in Mississippi State. His luck was out and during several days trailing he had not a single shot. His hosts, obviously embarrassed at the lack of sport, produced a captive young bear cub which Roosevelt contemptuously refused to kill. Clifford Berryman, a cartoonist on the paper, drew an amusing cartoon of the incident which was used to show the President's humanity. Describing the hunt to a friend, Roosevelt remarked that there had been plenty of bears but his hosts had turned the affair into a picnic and his failure had become a source of amusement to the 'comic press'. Berryman depicted the American President very well, but was not so skilled at animals, and his bear on a length of rope had little resemblance to a real grizzly. Was it this picture that sparked the idea of a toy?

This theory seemed to gain support in 1966 when, shortly after I had published a book on antique toys, I received a letter from Mr Benjamin F. Michtom, then Chairman of the Ideal Toy Corporation. Mr Michtom claimed that his father, Morris Michtom, was the first person to make a Teddy Bear and that I was quite wrong to suggest that jointed bears had first been produced by the German firm of Margarete Steiff. Morris Michtom originally came from Russia; maybe he was fond of bears, animals that figure so strongly in Russian folk tales and traditions. His son wrote:

13

It was my father who saw the cartoon in the *Washington Star*, November 18th 1902. My father and mother were in the toy business on a small scale and had a retail toy store. Mother made up the first sample bear cub. They made three more samples, sending one to President Roosevelt asking if he would object to our calling this toy bear cub 'Teddy Bear' in memory of the incident. The President wrote in longhand to my father that he did not think his name was worth much to the toy bear business, but we were welcome to use it. It was put on the market early in 1903. The first customer was Butler Bros. who took my father's output. In 1904 we added Sears Roebuck and between the two of them, they took the entire output of my father's factory. Thereafter the business expanded and became The Ideal Toy Corporation. One of the original Teddy Bears was presented by me to the great grandchildren of Theodore Roosevelt in Washington in 1963 to commemorate the sixtieth anniversary of the first Teddy Bear and the Roosevelts graciously donated the bear to the Smithsonian Institute where it now reposes.

There are some curious discrepancies in this story, and it seems more than careless that the original of the President's letter is now lost, together with a later letter which the Roosevelt family sent to his widow when Mr Michtom died in 1938. The bear in the Smithsonian does not look like a bear made as early as 1903, in either construction or material. Nevertheless, I am sure that the fundamentals of Mr Michtom's story are true, and that the cartoon did indeed give the name. The Michtoms achieved a remarkable success from their small beginnings in a little shop in New York. Famous stores such as Sears Roebuck and Butler Brothers guaranteed Morris Michtom's credit with the mills who supplied his materials, and in 1907 the Ideal Novelty and Toy Company became The Ideal Toy Corporation, one of the most eminent toy companies in the USA.

Theodore Roosevelt continued to use the little bear as a symbol in his election campaigns. It is especially interesting to find that the bear in an unpublished sketch called *On the Eve of War* that Clifford Berryman gave his father in 1917 looks even more like a toy Teddy Bear than a bear cub.

Despite his business acumen, Morris Michtom failed to do two important things – to take out a patent for his jointed Teddy Bear and to register a trademark. As a result many other manufacturers soon followed his lead and made similar Teddy Bears.

Right: An unpublished drawing by cartoonist Clifford Berryman of President 'Teddy' Roosevelt and Teddy Bear (or Teddy's bear).

The two American graphic Teddies of 1907 (shown above and right) are further evidence of Berryman's influence.

Four generations of
Teddies produced by the
world-famous German
toy-making firm of Steiff
– the other contender,
along with Morris
Michtom, in the battle
for first Teddy Bear
maker.

…And in the German Corner

The other principal contestant for the title of Original Teddy Maker is the German firm of Steiff, and the letters I received from Benjamin Michtom led me to do further research.

Margarete Steiff was born in the little town of Giengen-am-Brenz in Würtemburg in 1847. Early in life an attack of polio confined her to a wheelchair, and she amused herself with needlecraft, using scraps of felt from the family factory. As well as the more traditional things such as needle-cases and pin-cushions, she made up a few small stuffed elephants, which became very popular with visiting children. Her brother Fritz had the idea of selling some of her work in nearby markets and encouraged her to make a range of stuffed animals. Soon she became quite famous for her toys and began to take orders for them. By 1892 she had registered a trademark with a camel on wheels motif, and in 1898 she registered an elephant on wheels. The family combined forces in a small toy factory, and the firm remains in family hands today. Their larger animals were actually made to move on wheels so that a little child could ride them.

The Steiff version of the Teddy's origin is that Margarete made up a little jointed bear doll

Richard and Margarete Steiff, the aunt-and-nephew team that invented and produced the first Steiff Teddy in 1903.

designed by an artistic nephew, Richard. This animal, affectionately called 'Friend Petz' (*Petz* is the German equivalent of 'Bruin'), was shown among others at the Leipzig Trade Fair in 1903, and was ordered in large quantities by American buyers. The Steiffs believed that one person who patronized the little bear was Theodore Roosevelt's daughter Alice. Those responsible

Souvenirs of a lost
Europe: Steiff bears
photographed with their
proud owners on the eve
of the First World War.

Right: Now in the
process of being
restored, this well-loved
Steiff bear was made in
about 1910. It features
the large feet, elongated
paws and characteristic
expression of many
Steiff bears of the
period.

for her wedding reception at the White House were looking for appropriate table decorations. The caterer decided to dress up a number of little bears as huntsmen with rifles and set them among tents, with others as fishermen sitting around bowls of goldfish. The guests admired this ingenious reference to the favourite sport of the bride's father: 'What species do the bears belong to?', one guest jested with the President. 'You've got me there,' he answered, 'they must be the new species called TEDDY BEARS.'

It all sounds perfectly plausible. Much later, however, all those present denied that a display of this kind had been mounted, and the bride herself had no recollection of bears being present at the reception. Nonetheless, it does seem to be true that the Steiff family was making stuffed jointed bears in 1902 and 1903, at just the time that the *Washington Star* cartoon appeared.

An article in the German magazine *Illustrierte Zeitung* by a writer called Georg Queri gives an authentic historical account of production.

Left: Steiff bears were to be found in all the world's most celebrated department stores. This display of Steiff toys (including Teddies, on the left) took pride of place in the famous toy department of Gamage's, London, at Christmas, 1911.

Entitled *The Cradle of Teddy Bears*, it appeared in the September 1911 issue. Margarete Steiff herself had died in 1909, and Queri must have been a personal friend, since he uses the diminutive version of her name, 'Gretl'. Moreover, her nephews must have checked all he wrote, since they were still running the business very successfully. Georg Queri suggested that the bear 'doll' was an instant success with American buyers when it was shown at the Leipzig Fair because of the story of Roosevelt and the bear, and that it became a national symbol as a result.

The most interesting new feature of Queri's account, however, is his description of the artistic Steiff nephew Richard. Richard's father admired his sister Margarete's work and actively encouraged his son, who studied sculpture at the Stuttgart School of Arts and Crafts. Among his acquaintances was an animal-trainer in the famous Hagenbeck's Circus who did an attractive act with a performing bear. Richard was so enchanted with the good nature and behaviour of this beast that he sketched it in various exaggerated poses. It seems that this was indeed the origin of Margarete's bear, and

A quizzical old Steiff bear of about
1910 – complete with elongated
snout and humped back – expresses
a forceful personality.

Steiff was not the only German firm to produce Teddies; this acrobatic example was made in about 1910 by Gebrüder Bing of Nuremberg, better known to collectors for their mechanical tin toys. Here, their technical expertise has been well employed to produce this somersaulting stuffed bear; the spring-loaded mechanism is wound up by rotating the arms.

provides the reason why her earliest examples look so true to life, with the hump at the back of the neck, long paws, pointed snout and stitched claw lines. Some examples were made up with a muzzle strap and leading chain, just like a performing bear's.

Having discovered the origin of 'Friend Petz', I decided to look a little deeper into the history of the circus. In the last years of the 19th century, travelling circuses were especially popular in Europe, and many famous troupes of performing animals and their trainers toured with acrobats, equestrians and clowns. Hagenbeck's was one of the most famous. The original Herr Hagenbeck was a fish merchant in Hamburg who had the idea of exhibiting some of the seals he caught in his nets. His son Carl, who was renowned for his gentle methods and system of rewards for animals, developed the idea of animal-training. He established a famous zoo in natural surroundings at Stellingen near Dresden, dispensing with cages. Obviously he was concerned about the exploitation involved in training and transporting the larger, more unsuitable animals, and was, for instance, the first to introduce a metal cage in the ring for his

'big cat' acts when touring the USA in 1893. Hagenbeck insisted that an animal's affection had to be gained, and that cruelty could never induce the same respect and obedience as kindness. His reforms produced spectacular results. In 1909 he performed with 70 polar bears at the London Hippodrome, some of which were riding bicycles and playing on a specially designed see-saw!

It is a curious irony that Teddy Bears have come to represent all that is lovable in a toy animal, since in the wild bears are notoriously vicious, spiteful, mean and greedy. It is important to remember, however, that the Steiff image was inspired by one special bear, an amiable, clever Hagenbeck bear who waved to the crowd and gambolled to make the children laugh. The other crucial point is this: while Richard Steiff was studying circus acts he met another artist called Albert Schlopsnies, who designed some dolls for Gretl Steiff. I have often wondered about the curious little characters she made with a central seam and over-large feet, and this friendship provides the answer. Schlopsnies was a puppet-master, and the caricatures he drew represented puppet people –

Opposite: Almost certainly of
German origin, 'Roger' was made
in about 1930.

... AND IN THE GERMAN CORNER

puppets necessarily having weighted feet to enable them to swing, step and dance correctly. Frau Steiff turned the drawings into dolls using coloured felts and fabrics, and the article by Georg Queri has good photographs of set-pieces with animals and dolls made in the Steiff factory. There are clowns and elephants, the popular type of German percussion band with funny men in the circus ring, and a huge St Bernard dog entitled *Mein Liebling* ('my darling'), which endearment may describe either the dog or the curly-haired mite riding on its back. Another set-piece, described as Schlopsnies' design of the rehearsal at Sarrasani's Circus, includes little chairs, hoops, wagons and all the paraphernalia of the circus, as well as the performers. Sarrasani was a member of a wealthy Prussian family called Stosch, who ran away to join a circus. When he came into a large legacy in 1901 he founded his own fine circus and built a permanent ring in Dresden to house it.

Circuses in both Europe and the USA inspired many fine toys such as Schoenhut's Humpty Dumpty Circus with jointed figures of animals and clowns in turned wood. It is interesting to remember that Schoenhut too came originally

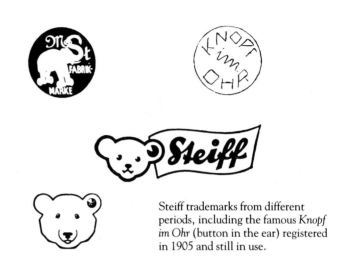

Steiff trademarks from different periods, including the famous *Knopf im Ohr* (button in the ear) registered in 1905 and still in use.

from Würtemburg and may have remembered boyhood circuses in Germany. Margarete Steiff's beautiful, hand-made soft toys set a fashion. Some of her designs were pirated, and for this reason she established the famous *Knopf im Ohr* ('Button in the Ear') trademark, a little metal stud clipped into the ear of her Teddies and animals to establish their identity. The mark was registered on May 13, 1905 in both Germany (where it was number 78878) and in England. The Steiff factory flourishes to this day and has fortunately preserved a valuable museum with family archives.

The French luxury stores of the early 1900s were quick to adopt the toy bear as a Christmas toy. This selection of bears, glimpsed in the pages of the catalogues of exclusive Parisian stores, displays an appropriate degree of bear-faced *chic*.

Teddies on the March

Now that the two principal claims for the first bear have been established, it is interesting to trace when and where the name was first used. In Europe jointed bears were pictured in Christmas bazaar catalogues in 1906, but were never called Teddy Bears. The pretty catalogue

issued by the fashionable Paris store Aux Trois Quartiers showed a bear made of 'soft woollen material' with articulated joints and wearing a small double-breasted suit with buttons and collar. It had a voice box and was recommended as a 'pillow for baby' – a 'novelty'. It was 18 inches (46 centimetres) tall and cost 6.9 francs (about a third of the price of the walking-talking bisque French doll also illustrated). Three years later another luxury French store, La Samaritaine, showed jointed bears in different sizes made of a natural-coloured plush. In addition to these Teddies (though they were only called *ours*, the French for bear), there was a novelty acrobatic bear on tumbling rings and a puss-in-boots. The bears were offered in white or beige. A bear chauffeur was on offer in 1913 at Bon Marché riding in a little lacquered automobile with headlamps and steering wheel, and the following year a bear made a catalogue cover for the first time, tucked in Santa Claus' sack.

In London, Gamage's Christmas catalogue in 1906 devoted a whole page to illustrations of felt- and plush-covered animals that were obviously made in the Steiff factory. These included a jointed bear, puss-in-boots, jointed

Teddies – rapidly becoming one of the world's most popular toys – were also a favourite subject for illustrators of the day. These sporting Teddies – up to every sporting trick in the book – were published in about 1909, the first heyday of the Teddy.

TEDDY AT TENNIS

TEDDY CYCLING

TEDDY AT CRICKET

Below: Four years after Berryman's cartoon, the London department store Gamage's featured a handsome jointed Steiff plush bear in its 1906 Christmas toy catalogue.

Below right: By 1907, Steiff had infiltrated the American market. This selection is from a wholesale catalogue offered by the American firm of L.H. Mace.

monkeys in fancy clothes, and jointed donkeys, elephants and a variety of dogs and cats. There is no mention of 'Teddy', but there are a number of Schlopsnies' quaint caricature people. Mr Gamage was a dedicated toy-lover and visited the Steiff factory to make his selection.

The earliest actual mentions of Teddy Bears by that name were in American trade magazines and mail-order catalogues, indicating that the name was bestowed in that country. One manufacturer in 1906 was using four thousand goats a week to provide wool for Teddies. In the same year *Playthings Magazine* announced that it was 'Bruin's Day', and in December carried an advertisement from E.I. Horsman, a New York importer, for 'best quality imported Teddy Bears'. By this time the name seems to have been in general use in the USA. Much plagiarizing went on, and some firms even brought in German workmen to reveal manufacturing secrets. In 1907 a New York store called L.H. Mace issued a mail-order catalogue, one page of which showed Teddy Bears, plush bears and elephants and Stieff's Bears (*sic*). The German bears came in three colours: golden brown, white and seal brown and were almost

Left: America fights back with the 'Real Thing' – American-made bears advertised in *Playthings Magazine* of 1907.

twice as expensive as their American-made fellows. The largest size (20 inches; 51 centimetres) cost no less than $66 a dozen or $5.50 each – for which money you could buy a good sledge or tricycle from the same catalogue.

A Joyful Easter
Cheery greetings come t[...]
Their happy part on East[...]

A Happy Easter

WHO ARE YOU ?

SEAL-SKIN JACKETS
ALTERED TO
THE LATEST FASHION

A MERRY CHRISTMAS

Before the First World War,
greetings cards – both humorous and
sentimental – were quick to reflect
the craze of Teddies. Christmastide
Teddies were especially popular, but
Easter, too, could tempt a shy
Teddy out of his shell (see above).

Here's something to love
and something to tease,
Something to cuddle and something to
squeeze,

Someone
who'll stick thro' st...
A dear little, cute lit...
Bro...

H.B. London, W...

Here's something to love
and something to tease,
Something to cuddle and something to
squeeze,

...ro' storm and fair,
...ute little
...Brown Teddy Bear.

Fully Protected.

We have secured exclusive control of the
Electric Bright Eye Teddy Bears
and in addition to the bears will offer to the trade a
complete line of Electric Eye Animals in greatly
improved styles

The Real
Novelty in
Bears,
Tige Dogs, Cats
Elephants
and other
Jointed Animals
with
Electric Eyes

RABBITS
FOR THE
EASTER
TRADE
ORDER NOW

Patented Feb 19th, 1907

BAKER & BIGLER CO.
SOLE MANUFACTURERS
643 Broadway and 77-79 Bleecker St., Cor. Bway., New York

MOVING PICTURE TEDDIES

PATENTED JAN. 15, 1907
PATENTED JUNE 25, 1907

Left: *Moving Picture Teddies.* Now
highly sought after, this 1907
American children's novelty book
was a typical product of the
international Teddies craze.

Above: Advertisement for the
'Electric Bright Eye Teddy Bear',
made by Baker & Bigler of New
York in 1908.

Top: Early cut-out novelty Teddies
– made from velvet and mounted
on postcards.

32

The Craze for Teddies

By 1907, Teddy Bear enthusiasm had reached manic proportions. Besides the actual bears themselves, there were boxed games such as *Teddy's Bear Hunt* and ranges of clothes especially for Teddy boys and Teddy girls, and the Teddy image was painted on china tea sets, metal buckets and rubber stamps. In addition there were numerous types of Teddy paper cut-outs, books, postcards, notepaper and card games; carts and carriages and boats and automobiles specially made for Teddies; and a variety of novelty Teddies that growled or squeaked. One Teddy even had eyes that lit up when its right paw was shaken; this was known as the Electric Bright Eye Teddy Bear.

Anyone in the business of making Teddy Bears was successful, but especially that German firm of Steiff in the little town of Giengen-am-Brenz. It produced over 900,000 bears in 1907, employing 400 factory hands and no less than 1800 women out-workers. At an exhibition staged at Worthing Museum in Sussex, England, in 1965, people were invited to lend their old Teddy Bears. The aim was to make a census of dates and types. The result was amazing, demonstrating above all how people adored and

This American paper Teddy cut-out set was produced in about 1908. Teddy 'in the raw' was provided with a variety of entertaining outfits in which he could be dressed and given an individual identity.

A 1965 exhibition in Worthing, England, demonstrated how people cherished and adored their old bears. Above and right: Steiff bears from the 1903 to 1909 vintage shown in the exhibition. (See also page 33).

Far right: Teddy tenderness: affecting scenes in the Teddy hospital.

Ain't Babies Rough

Oh, Doctor! say he will get well,
We Nurses work like horses;
We'll make him sound as any bell,
We girls who wear Red Crosses.
H.M.B.

cherished their old bears. Some Teddies, it was discovered, dated to 1903, 1904 and 1905 and had documented family histories attached; all the veterans were undoubtedly made by Steiff. It was this discovery that especially infuriated Benjamin Michtom, as I found in our later correspondence. But it is a fact that Britain imported German bears, not American ones.

A few doubters had misgivings about the popularity of the Teddy Bear, especially, one

Bearing the scars of an eventful career, this multicoloured bear of about 1910 has a cinnamon coloured head and legs but mixed coloured plush on his body and arms. Judging by his expression, he's a bit worried by the difference.

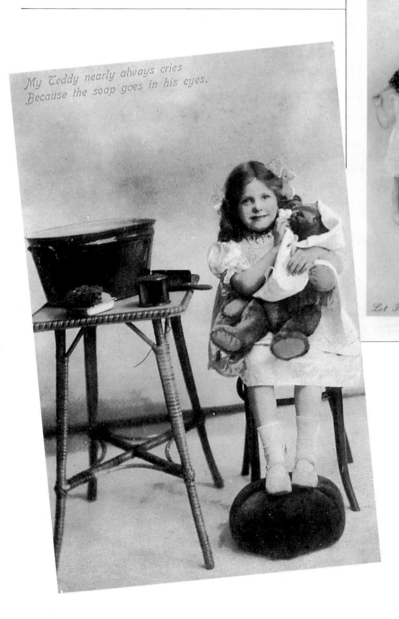

*My Teddy nearly always cries
Because the soap goes in his eyes.*

Teddies soon broke out of the 'toys for boys' category and threatened to displace dolls from the affections of girls. Dedicated doll-lovers were horrified: here we see Teddies cossetted, bathed, dressed and generally cared for. On occasion, Teddies might come to drive dolls still further down the pecking order, as in the picture opposite by illustrator Lawson Wood, in which Teddy cossets the family doll.

Let Teddy be bathed first Mummy!

THE MORNING BATH.
*"Teddy-bear cannot be seen
Until his face is nice and clean."*

08873/5

presumes, the makers of dolls! Although Teddies were thought of as toys for boys, it was soon discovered that little girls liked them as well. In *The Doll Book* (1908), one of the earliest American doll-collecting books, Laura Starr quoted a chauvinistic outburst, intended to keep little girls (and Teddy Bears) in their rightful place, from the *Western Editor*, which was, I believe, a trade magazine.

It is enough to make a perfect lady of a doll mad. The dear little girls who have always cried for dolls at Christmas, are this year crying for Teddy Bears, and dolls are left on the shelves to cry the paint off their pretty cheeks because of the neglect. So great is the demand for Teddy Bears, which range in price from ninety eight cents to twelve dollars, that the factories can't keep up the supply, and what makes it still more alarming is that factories are supplying sweaters, overalls, jackets and so forth, for the bears. Will it be as pretty a sight when a little girl mothers a bear as when she mothers a doll? Well, we guess not. We are on the side of the dolls, and are ready to preside at an indignation meeting of dolls, baby dolls, boy dolls and lady dolls at any time they call the meeting. We are not much of a talker, but we are this much better talkers than a doll: we can talk without being punched in the stomach.

By 1912 some of the early novelty was wearing off, and Teddy Bears were not such a fad. In 1914 the German bears completely lost their popularity and there was sterner stuff to think about than toy bears. During the First World War, some British toy-makers did better for the very reason that people only 'bought British', and in the 1920s they surged ahead, producing very fine toys.

A honey-coloured bear of classic proportions, bought in Harrods, London's yet-to-be fashionable store, in 1905. He has a flat head, shaved nose, long arms, turned-in paws, shapely legs and big feet.

The Mystery Deepens

In 1954 the trade magazine *Games and Toys* published an article by Mr H.E. Bryant, Chairman of the British Toy Manufacturing Association, that added yet another element of mystery to the parentage of the Teddy Bear. Referring to the output of one of the most famous British firms, Farnell's, he said:

> It is interesting to note that these toys were made from rabbit skins and took the form of toy monkeys, rabbits etc and from these beginnings came the manufacture of the ever popular Teddy Bear. We are all fully aware that when an unnamed Englishman invented the idea, it was offered to Margarete Steiff who immediately saw the possibilities of such a production in England. The idea was presented to a Yorkshire manufacturer of pile fabrics who visualized the possibilities of a plush to be used by the toy trade and in consequence of this, toys of all sorts began to appear, designed for and using this type of material. Farnell's took every advantage of this development and by their own new methods invaded the original home of toy makers by exporting quantities to Germany. The man responsible for the distribution in that country was one familiarly known over here, named Jos. Susskind.

It would seem that what we have here is a German bear made with Yorkshire plush and endowed with an American name. I understand

Two photographs of 'Bruin', made by the British firm of Farnell in 1920. The identical model to Christopher Robin Milne's Pooh, also made by Farnell in the same year, Bruin was originally owned by a Farnell employee; a cherished family bear, he has been passed down through the generations.

And that's the
sort of fellows we are.

Ask Father!

Twixt hope and fear.

Two's company
Three's a crowd.

I shan't speak first.

that the name of the mysterious Englishman was Robinson. Maybe somewhere in the Steiff archives are letters that prove the link.

My information on the history of Farnell's comes chiefly from the daughter of a woman who worked for the company. The Farnell toy business began in 1840, and in 1870 it was run by Agnes Farnell and her brother J.K. Farnell at the family home, Elm House, Acton, in West London. By the end of the First World War a private company with £10,000 capital was established and a small factory called the Alpha Works built. Teddy Bears on the Steiff pattern were produced with beautiful plush material, as well as monkeys, elephants and a fine range of dogs: terriers, spaniels, scotties, sheep dogs, chows and St Bernards. Although the cartoon favourite Felix the Cat was a successful line, the firm's speciality remained high-class Teddy Bears and soft animals. Harrods was one of its best customers, and it was a Farnell bear that became a national – and international – celebrity soon after it was bought in 1920 for a rather special little boy called Christopher Robin Milne. My informant, who was born at about the same time, was given an identical model by her

Left: The real-life Christopher Robin Milne with his Farnell Teddy Bear, Winnie-the-Pooh (formerly known as Edward), and Kanga in the Hollow Tree House at Cotchford Farm, Sussex, England, in about 1926.

mother, and still has scraps of the original silky plush used for Teddies and the mottled plush from which Tiggers were made.

In 1934 a disastrous fire destroyed the Farnell home and damaged their factory, and Agnes Farnell died soon afterwards. J.C. Janisch, a director of Farnell's, started up a rival soft toy company known as Merrythought in Shropshire. This famous firm with its 'Wishbone' trademark still exists, and still manufactures Teddies. The finance for the new company was provided by W.J. Holmes and Laxton Mohair Spinners of Oakwood in Yorkshire (the plush-makers), and eventually Holmes' son ran the company.

Left and above: L. Frank Baum, the author of *The Wizard of Oz* and subsequent Oz stories, peopled his unique 'world of Oz' with fantastic characters and creations. Teddy Bears were not omitted. Left: A determined Teddy strides forth in *The Tin Woodman of Oz* (1918). Above: The Big Lavender Bear, intent on action, carries the Little Pink Bear with him in *The Lost Princess of Oz* (1917).

Right: An impressive 'hug' of little Teddies illustrated in *The Family of Little Brown Bears* story that ran in the 1920s *Little Dots* annual.

Literary and Artistic Teddies

My own first Teddy Bears were the smallest and the cheapest obtainable in the 1920s. No more than 3 inches (8 centimetres) high, they fitted well into the splendid home-made dolls' house that my mother and twin brothers built and furnished at the end of the First World War. Besides the natural fawn and white varieties, I recall that one could buy pale pink and pale blue ones. Children of that period had no problem understanding stories of Teddy Bears that talked, dressed and had wild adventures. The literary output was enormous. Hardly a children's annual of the 1920s appeared without some nursery story which included a Teddy or a Bear family. *Little Dots*, a monthly twopenny periodical with a gentle Sunday School flavour, ran 'The Family of the Little Brown Bears' told and illustrated by Chris Temple. The bears, it might be noticed,

'Sick Teddy' and 'Teddy Bear Tea Party': the author's own first Teddies, made and bought in the 1920s.

were completely masculine: Marmaduke, Clarence, Cuthbert, Archibald, Frederick, Algernon and the Little One – all obvious Teddy Bear names.

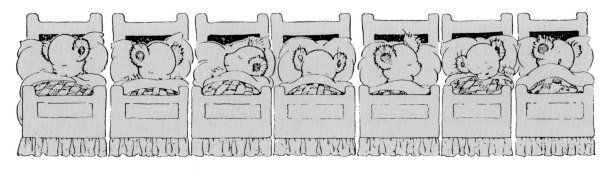

43

The Big Lavender Bear

CHAPTER 15

It was a pleasant place to wander in and the two travelers were proceeding at a brisk pace when suddenly a voice shouted

"Halt!"

They looked around in surprise, seeing at first one at all. Then from behind a tree there stepp brown fuzzy bear, whose head came about as hi Cayke's waist — and Cayke was a small woman. bear was chubby as well as fuzzy; his body wa

198

The Little Pink Bear

CHAPTER 16

"One Person and one Freak," said the big Lavender Bear, when he had carefully examined the strangers.

"I am sorry to hear you call poor Cayke the Cookie Cook a Freak," remonstrated the Frogman.

"She is the Person," asserted the King. "Unless I am mistaken, it is you who are the Freak."

The Frogman was silent, for he could not truthfully deny it.

206

The Little Pink Bear Speaks Truly

CHAPTER 24

For several minutes they all stood staring at the black spot on the canvas of the Magic Picture, wondering what it could mean.

"P'raps we'd better ask the little Pink Bear about zma," suggested Trot.

"Pshaw!" said Button-Bright, "he don't know ything."

He never makes a mistake," declared the King.

293

The American author Frank Baum followed his hugely successful children's fantasy *The Wonderful Wizard of Oz* (1900) with less famous titles based on the same mythology. One, *The Lost Princess of Oz* (1917), provides some interesting documentary evidence about contemporary Teddy Bears. The story, which is tame enough, concerns a city peopled by toy bears. One, a brown bear on guard duty,

… was chubby as well as fuzzy; his body was even puffy, while his legs and arms seemed jointed at the knees and elbows and fastened to his body by pins or rivets. His ears were round in shape and stuck out in a comical way, while his round black eyes were bright and sparkling as beads.

Challenged by another character, who guesses that he is stuffed with sawdust, he retaliates indignantly: 'I am stuffed with a very good

44

Left: Chapter openers from the first edition of L. Frank Baum's *The Lost Princess of Oz* (1917), one of the Oz stories in which Teddy Bears play an important part.

Right: An American embossed depiction of 'Teddy B' – perhaps a relative of Teddy B created by American author Seymour Eaton in 1905. (See page 46.)

Below: Big Teddy and Little Teddy (missing a leg and an arm) in one of Honor C. Appleton's illustrations for Mrs Cradock's Josephine books, published in Britain from 1917.

quality of curled hair and my skin is the best plush that was ever made.' Reigning over this kingdom of bears at Bear Centre is a beautiful lavender-hued Royal Bear with 'bright pink eyes'. His treasured magician is a tiny Pink Bear, which, when wound up by a key, can give the correct answer to any question and can even walk mechanically. The Royal Bear declares proudly that there is not another magic bear like this in the world. Presumably the author modelled his characters on coloured and mechanical bears and passed them as reference to his artist John R. Neill.

Some of the first Teddy stories were the Josephine Books, written by Mrs H.C. Cradock and illustrated by Honor C. Appleton. Published from 1917 onwards by Blackie & Son, they were based on Mrs Cradock's own small daughter's toys. The characters included Big Teddy and Little Teddy, who had lost one arm and one leg – a common occurrence before joints were safety-made.

While many ordinary books featured the type of Teddy that could be bought off a shop shelf, character Teddies relied on the individual charm lent by the artist. Among the earliest of these

R.K. Culver illustrated many of Seymour Eaton's stories of the Roosevelt Bears, Teddy-B and Teddy-G. Favourite American literary Teddies, the well-travelled duo are shown here leaving on a European adventure and arriving in England to a welcome from no less a host than Edward VII.

Over the years, the Roosevelt Bears were involved in a wide range of activities and adventures. Whether

were two who started life in a strip cartoon in the USA: Teddy-B and Teddy-G (the initials stood for Brown and Gray). Created by Seymour Eaton in 1905, they appeared in several books and were illustrated by a succession of artists (especially R.K. Culver) and looked like dressed-up Grizzlies with real teeth and claws. Eaton claimed that Roosevelt and his sons enjoyed them; certainly the books were highly popular and are still sought by collectors.

John Hassall, the famous poster artist, was one of the first artists to use a Teddy Bear character in Britain; he probably worked from an actual toy as well, since his daughter Joan, the famous wood-engraver, was five years old when he published *Echo, Echo*. The curious text concerns a rather intellectual, stringy, athletic-looking bear who shared unlikely adventures with Greek Gods such as Mercury and the children who owned him.

strolling down Fifth
Avenue or taking rather more
strenuous forms of exercise, their
lives are recorded here in an
entertaining graphic series from
around 1907.

No. 15. The Roosevelt Bears in New York City.
" They spent some days in seeing the town ;
Doing Fifth Avenue up and down."

Roosevelt Bear paw marks.
On the right, that of
Teddy-G; on the far right,
that of Teddy-B.

No. 12. The Roosevelt Bears Take an Auto Ride.
" " We've broken something," said TEDDY.
" It's underneath, get down and TEDD..."

No. 13. The Roosevelt Bears at Harvard
" These gowns and caps and scrolls you ...
We give you now as your degree."

No. 9. The Roosevelt Bears in the Department Store.
" It was worth a trip a mile to see
This paper package marked TEDDY-G."

47

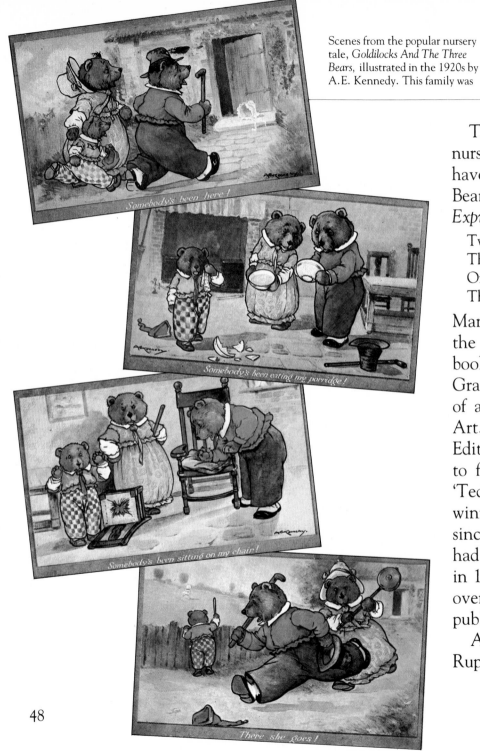

Scenes from the popular nursery tale, *Goldilocks And The Three Bears*, illustrated in the 1920s by A.E. Kennedy. This family was perhaps the original inspiration for Mr Bear, Mrs Bear and Rupert (see opposite).

Somebody's been here!

Somebody's been eating my porridge!

Somebody's been sitting on my chair!

There she goes!

The tale of The Three Bears is a traditional nursery favourite with children, and must surely have engendered the first stories of Rupert the Bear, who began as a strip cartoon in the *Daily Express* on November 8, 1920.

> Two Jolly Bears lived in a wood
> Their little son lived there too
> One day his Mother sent him off
> The marketing to do.

Mary Tourtel, who wrote the verses and drew the pictures, had already illustrated children's books, notably the Dumpy books published by Grant Richards in 1902. She came from a family of artists and trained at Canterbury School of Art. Her husband, Herbert Tourtel, was Night Editor of the *Daily Express*, and she was invited to find a character to compete with Folkard's 'Teddy Tail' in the rival *Daily Mail*. She found a winner in Rupert, who has been a favourite ever since. Because of failing eyesight, Mary Tourtel had to give up her column in 1935 and she died in 1948, at the age of 75. The frame was taken over by Alfred Bestall and was eventually published in book form and in coloured annuals.

As a child of the 1920s, I always thought of Rupert as black and white – just as he appeared

48

in the newspaper. I was amazed to see him in a red jersey and yellow check trousers, though I do not think I ever questioned how a little bear could have real little hands with fingers and thumbs and presumably real little feet with toes inside his neat shoes! In essence the humanized Rupert was a good little boy with pleasant manners and a happy nature. In later years his

English picture book hero, Rupert the Bear, has now been alive – and kicking – for over 60 years. Here he is shown with one of his greatest fans, Paul McCartney, on the record sleeve for *We All Stand Together*, and with his mother, Mrs Bear, in one of Alfred Bestall's *Daily Express* frames.

Right and below: Bear as epic hero. Rupert on the trail of more adventures in the popular and colourful *Daily Express* annuals.

Rupert and the Spring Adventure

RUPERT DISCOVERS AN IMP

He runs awhile, then glances round,
For he has heard a funny sound.

As through the bushes Rupert peers
A tiny Imp of Spring appears.

The imp explains, " Our plants won't grow
Because there's trouble down below."

Now Rupert's quick to understand
And off they scamper hand in hand.

Rupert takes the shortest way to Pong-Ping's home, but he has not got far when a strange sound makes him turn. "It's coming from over there by that tree," he whispers. "And surely there's a wisp of smoke coming from that one, too!" He walks across and is just peering more closely when a small, neat figure shoots upwards through the smoke right in front of him, looking very frightened and calling for help. Rupert is so startled that he nearly falls down. When he has got over his fright Rupert gazes at the queer little stranger. "Why, you're one of the Imps of Spring, aren't you?" he says. "Yes, I am," cries the Imp. "And we're in dreadful trouble. There's an awful thing down there burning the roots of the trees, and if it isn't driven out we shall have no spring flowers round here at all!" "The dragon again!" shouts Rupert. "I'm just going to ask Pong-Ping about it. Come with me." And together they race off faster than ever.

72

50

Right: E.H. Shepard, the British artist used by A.A. Milne to illustrate his Winnie-the-Pooh books, bequeathed his original sketches to the Victoria & Albert Museum, London, in 1969. This 1924 study shows Christopher Robin's own Teddy, Winnie-the-Pooh. The eventual model for all the A.A. Milne books was Growler, a Teddy belonging to the artist's son.

Christopher Robin's Pooh bear (as he began life in 1924) E H Shepard

adventures became more exotic, involving magic and flying saucers. But the good image has remained, and all is still well in Rupert's world.

It is intriguing to discover that the famous Teddy Bear that belonged to Christopher Robin was originally called Edward. In 'Teddy Bear', A.A. Milne's first poem about him, illustrated by E.H. Shepard, he is bewailing his fat shape. This is the ninth in the series of poems, *When We Were Very Young*, and was published in *Punch* on February 13, 1924 and subsequently as a book. At that time Christopher Robin was only three and a half years old, and the bear had hardly changed since it was bought for his first birthday at Harrods.

Shepard loved children and had two of his own, a girl, Mary, and a boy, Graham. It was Graham's bear, Growler (vintage 1906), who was the model for Pooh. Growler was a Steiff bear, while Edward was made by Farnell, but in looks and shape and size they were very similar. Edward later became Winnie-the-Pooh in Milne's particular brand of whimsy. Winnie was the name of Christopher Robin's favourite bear at London Zoo, and Pooh was his name for a swan he fed with bread on the pond. The original of Pooh, together with his friends Kanga (Roo, the baby, is lost), Tigger and Eeyore sit in a glass cabinet in the New York office of the publisher E.P. Dutton. When they travel, as befits such celebrities, they fly British Airways and are received in the VIP lounge.

In the 1920s and early 1930s, Christopher Robin and the Pooh stories were enormously popular; small boys were dressed in his style in smocked tunics and had square bobbed hair. In 1966, when Walt Disney decided that the books were suitable material for a cartoon, the child and the toys were so completely transformed that

Left and below: The Bear of Very Little Brain in action in *The House at Pooh Corner*, published in 1928. Below left: A reflective Pooh pens a poem in *The House at Pooh Corner*. Opposite: E.H. Shepard illustrated A.A. Milne's poem, *Teddy Bear*, in 1924. Then unknown, Winnie-the-Pooh lived under the simple soubriquet 'Teddy Bear'. The poem was included in the anthology, *When We Were Very Young* (1924).

British admirers could not recognize him, and it was realized how weak the text was without the drawings. Nevertheless, the change was necessary for an American public who would have had little understanding of a middle-class nanny-run nursery in the London of 1920. Curiously when the American-style models returned to Britain, the result was a new vogue for the original books. In fact, E.H. Shepard had

53

Opposite: An historical curiosity: this German-made bear of about 1920 wears an expression exactly like that of E.H. Shepard's Pooh.

already published a coloured-plate edition in 1957, *The World of Christopher Robin*, with all its original magic.

Each age seems to find its special bear, and one suspects that in the 20th century the appeal of the Teddy is partly the result of the 'small family' syndrome. The huge families of Victorian times needed such companions less. A current famous literary Teddy is Paddington, who was invented by Michael Bond and originally illustrated by Peggy Fortnum. Bond bought Paddington at Selfridges as a Christmas present for his wife and published the first story in 1956.

Opposite and below: Michael Bond's Paddington – star of numerous adventures and famed for his duffel coat and penchant for marmalade sandwiches – arrived from Peru on Paddington Station in 1956. Since then he has become one of the best known and loved of all literary bears.

Please look after this bear thank you.

Paddington emerged as a Peruvian Teddy Bear dressed in a curious outfit of floppy felt hat, duffle coat and Wellington boots and lost on Paddington Station, London – hence his name.

In Britain he appeared on television much later in this guise and has emigrated, unaltered, to the USA. Recently he made his debut as a computer game to teach youngsters their sums!

SOOTY'S GARAGE

Left: British TV star Sooty prepares to fill up Sweep's car with 'Sooto' – a somewhat dubious brand of fuel. Harry Corbett's characters were British television favourites in the 1950s; today the show, now performed by Corbett's son, still provides the opportunity for much Teddy fun and games.

Below: Andy Pandy and his Teddy Bear have been popular in many corners of the globe for over thirty years. They made their first appearance on British television's *Watch with Mother* in the early 1950s.

Opposite: 'Chad', the Teddy chosen to advertise Bear Brand stockings of Chicago, was made at the British Chad Valley toy factory in about 1955. Sold recently at Sotheby's in London, Chad went for a high price appropriate to his unique career.

Media Teddies

Television has produced its own Teddy Bear characters especially for the under-fives (though a lot of grown-ups watch too). Andy Pandy first appeared in 1950, a little clown boy with Looby Loo the rag doll and a mischievous Teddy known simply as Teddy. The Teddy was made by Chad Valley and was especially adapted with loosely-strung limbs to enable him to perform as a puppet. Stories told by Maria Bird featured this endearing little character, who had a lot of simple props such as baskets and boxes, buckets and swings. The Andy Pandy costume (with accompanying Teddy) was a favourite fancy dress for small children, and many songs and books were based on the programme.

Hardly less popular in the same years was the glove puppet Sooty. Sooty was a golden bear with black ears and a smudge nose originally bought by the entertainer Harry Corbett on the North Pier, Blackpool, to take home and amuse his children. In the familiar pattern of the family toy that becomes a national pet, Sooty's naughty behaviour soon captured a large audience; with his dog-friend Sweep he indulged in a kind of Teddy Bear slapstick comedy, with things generally being broken, spilt or downright wrecked. My own children used to chorus 'Ooooooh Sooty!' whenever something got knocked over at table. Sooty has survived to the second generation, and Corbett's son now performs the show in Britain.

In 1907, when the Teddy Bear craze was at its height, Teddy Bears were given away as advertising premiums, and ever since the toy has remained a popular advertising mascot. Bear Brand Stockings of Chicago began with a Grizzly Bear trademark, but later settled for a Chad Valley bear. Mrs Ford, wife of one of the

Below: 'Mischka', the Teddy mascot chosen by the Russians for the Olympic Games held in Moscow in 1980.

Opposite: 'Alfred', a bear with a memorably mischievous expression, was made by the British Chad Valley toy company in the 1920s.

directors, visited the English factory to choose 'Chad', who was used, complete with top hat and cane, to advertise nylon stockings in shops throughout the USA. An example sold recently for a high price at Sotheby's in London. 'Cosy' was the bear mascot of the Coal Utilization Company in the 1960s, gracing otherwise stark-looking coal-merchants' windows. He was intended to extol the virtues of solid fuel heating.

Although the bear is as symbolic an animal for Russia as the lion is for England, there has never been a Red Ted. Bears often appear in old Russian folk tales and fairy stories, and it was natural enough for 'Mischka' to have been chosen as the mascot of the Moscow Olympic Games in 1980. 'Mischka' bore a curious resemblance to the first little cub in the Berryman cartoon, with round ears and a Disney-like pattern, and the 5-ring Olympic hoops worn as a belt at its waist. Unhappily, the boycott of the Games meant that the toy was less than popular.

All sorts of bears now appear as personal mascots and team-leaders at television quizzes, football games and almost any contest one likes to mention. The curious thing is that the Teddy has assumed its own special character. Despite the fact that real bears have unpleasant natures and are potentially dangerous, Teddies are friendly, cuddly and everyone's favourite. Both Pooh and Paddington share a greedy predilection for sweet food, Pooh with his store of honey pots, Paddington with a marmalade sandwich stored in his hat for emergencies. The name is even used to describe a nice old buffer, jolly and

comfortable. And we have no less than that unpredictable star, the late Elvis Presley, singing that he wanted to be his girl's Teddy Bear, with a chain around his neck – which takes us right back to the beginning, when Richard Steiff sat sketching a performing bear in a circus and his aunt created a performing 'bear doll' for little boys.

Left: Bears have a worldwide popularity as mascots. This appealing example bears the coat of arms of Barnet Council, London, on his front.

Below and right: It is a regrettable fact that bears have a greedy predilection for sweet food. Pooh and Paddington are, disgracefully, no exception to this rule!

FULL UP!

Once established, Teddies came to be made in all shapes and sizes. The two larger examples in this group were made by the famous German toy manufacturer Schuco. The dressed bear has a sheet metal casing covered with cloth; his hat and trousers are an integral part of his body. Made in 1937, he still bears his original trade label. Nose in air, the perky pale yellow plush bear's head movement is operated by pulling his tail. He dates from about 1948.

Teddies in the Making

At one time manufacturers used real fur and skin for soft toys and stuffed them with waste material such as clippings of flock. The early Farnell animals were made in this way. Construction improved with the introduction of good-quality wool plush, and, when 'squeaker' or 'growler' voice boxes were inserted, a less fibrous stuffing such as sawdust or wood wool was used. Today,

materials must be hygienic, and eye attachments and fastenings must pass stringent safety regulations.

During the 1960s the firm of Wendy Boston displayed a huge Teddy going through a washing-machine as an advertisement at the annual Toy Trade Fair. Alresford Toys of the Hampshire town of the same name, the source of some of the finest modern bears, uses flame-resistant fabric fur and carded (washable) polyester fibre for a resilient filling. The most modern bear of all must be the 'Rockabye Bear', in which an electronic device simulates the sounds within a woman's womb, reproducing this soothing music to waft baby off to sleep.

I'VE A PAIN IN MY SQUEAKER.

Far left: An exciting development in Teddy technology was the 'squeaker' or 'growler'. The new squeakers even received publicity on contemporary postcards – but the invention does not seem to have met with approval here.

Left: This unique novelty Teddy has a concealed secret. Remove his head and his tummy opens up to reveal a hidden powder compact.

LOOK AND SEE
WHAT "TEDDY" BEARS.

From

Pier & Sands.

Registered.

A MORNING DIP.

Teddies were a favourite topic for illustration by postcard artists. Teddy postcards were eagerly sought and sent on both sides of the Atlantic, seaside subjects sent from holiday being among the most popular. Seaside Teddy novelties abounded; the famous printing firm of Raphael Tuck, which described itself as 'publishers to their Majesties the King and Queen', included the example shown here (top left) in its series 'Little Bears'.

Graphic Teddies

There are as many claims for the inauguration of the picture postcard as for the invention of the Teddy Bear, and the truth seems to be that postcards evolved in various European countries and for various reasons. Fundamentally, it was the development of new printing techniques and the rapid advance of photographic reproduction that made postcards both popular and numerous. The rapid extension of the railway network, making travel so much easier, also led to the custom of sending postcards. In Germany during the 1870s the *Grüss Aus* or 'Greetings from' type was a favourite holiday card. There was a little vignette of a local place – either in the country or in the city – and a space at the bottom for a few words of greeting and a name to be added. Colour printing processes and hand-tinting gradually replaced black and white or sepia cards and made the scenes more attractive and truer to life. In 1894 the British Post Office allowed postcards to be sent with a halfpenny stamp, and by 1900 cards were being produced with the reverse side divided by a line to allow both message and address to be written.

The postal service was so speedy that a card sent off in the morning would reach a nearby destination that afternoon. 'Drop me a line' was as normal a request as 'give me a ring' is now. Soon numerous producers were competing to produce fancy cards, and a craze for collecting them in albums grew up. As people travelled further afield on trains, bicycles and cars and boasted of the places they visited, view cards became especially popular. When the *Picture Postcard Magazine* was first issued for collectors in 1900, Raphael Tuck, the famous fine art publishers, organized a competition with a prize of £1000 for the largest collection of their cards, to consist only of those that had passed through the post.

The firm of Raphael Tuck was founded by a Prussian businessman named Tuch who was born near Breslau, lost his money after the Austro-Prussian War and emigrated to London with his large family of eight children. Tuch set up a small shop to sell pictures and fancy printed paper objects, and introduced German printing methods to the fine art business. He changed his name from Tuch to Tuck between 1866 and 1870 and, assisted by his three sons, Gustaf, Adolf and Herman, built up a highly prestigious company producing decorative cards and

Left: 'Can you bear it?', the first of several un-bear-able puns to appear on this delightful series of early American cards, designed to prove that the average Teddy's week is no less arduous than that of the average human. The same could be said for the activity depicted below – this time on a British card.

GRAPHIC TEDDIES

reproductions. A fine factory was built in Moorfields, London, and a Royal Warrant was received from Queen Victoria, who used vast quantities of their Christmas cards. When picture postcards became popular at the end of the century Tuck was at the forefront, selling pretty subjects especially for children, as well as colourful annuals and story books. Raphael Tuck died in 1900 but the firm continued under his sons.

In 1906 an article by J. Kennedy Maclean on picture postcards in the London magazine *Quiver* claimed that 630 million postcards were sent by post every year. Maclean interviewed Adolph Tuck, the son of Raphael Tuck, to find out why they were popular. Tuck explained that the custom had originated in Germany and that he realized that picture postcards would be a great success. When he met the Postmaster General to ask that cards should be produced in the larger continental size, Tuck received forward information that permission would be granted from November 1, 1898, and produced a selection accordingly. They were not enthusiastically received, but after the competition trade increased dramatically. Tuck used his own

BLOW HARDER!

VIB (Very Important Bear) Teddy Edward (see also page 74) frequently travels abroad (here to Mount Everest) and, when at home, frequents the Houses of Parliament.

There he might expect to meet Humphrey (centre), a bear who currently resides at 10 Downing Street, London, with his owner, one Margaret Thatcher.

photographers to make artistic studies of places all over the world, and about a dozen artists produced copyright designs. Tuck estimated output in Germany in 1905 at 1161 million cards, and thought that they were used as an educational tool. Portraits were also popular (but there was a 'limited sale' for bishops). Royal portraits were also much in demand, as well as illuminated hymn cards; these involved an immense amount of production work.

Among the well-known British firms were C.W. Faulkner, which started in about 1900 and used a spray of ivy leaves as a trademark; Valentine & Sons of Dundee, who first produced

Left and above: One of a sought-after series of Teddy postcards produced in 1907 by the British firm C.W. Faulkner. The company's ivy leaf trademark is shown above.

postcards in 1897; and Bamforths from Holmfirth, Yorkshire, a family firm still in existence. Founded in about 1870, Bamforths originally specialized in lantern slides for magic lanterns and had the clever idea of making up their tableaux with family members and local people in costume. They did the same to illustrate song titles and hymns on postcards, and sentimental subjects for children. The example, shown on this page, of 'Mary with her little bear behind' is typical, and one wonders if the young lady concerned ever lived it down!

Teddies are no strangers to confusion. Bamforth's famous postcard, 'Mary with her little bear behind', was issued in 1908.

May you carry everything before you

'May Life's Pathway be smooth for you

All Good Luck to You

Complete with optimistic messages, these cards – available on both sides of the Atlantic in around 1910 – no doubt filled many a home with cheer.

Since the introduction of coloured cards coincided so closely with the craze for Teddies, they are often depicted, and were a favourite ploy in child portraiture. Many gorgeous bears are shown seated with equally charming children on fancy settees, high chairs or fur rugs. On their first birthday in 1907, my twin brothers were given bears to clutch, but, being the potential sportsmen they were, they looked upon it as an 'hurling-the bear' contest and, despite their angelic looks, managed to disrupt the group.

Commercially, the 'child-with-bear' group was a best-seller, but as cheap amateur photography developed it also became possible to buy packs of printed postcards with sensitized surfaces on which a contact print could be made of your own subject – your own children and their Teddies, for instance.

Postcard-collecting was very popular between 1900 and 1914, and often on the back of some pretty card there is just the message 'Thought you would like this for your album'. Gradually, the standard of printing deteriorated, and, as more and more publishers entered the market, cheeky and vulgar types such as McGill's 'seaside' postcards increased. There were comic

Below: 'Hurling the bear': the author's twin brothers and elder cousin with the remains of their first Teddy in the foreground. Reproduced on a postcard, this is a shocking example of 'bear abuse'!

Right: A vast Teddy – who would be able to protect himself with ease – forms the focus of another delightful 'child-with-bear' photograph.

I've so many things to carry,
It's not strange I've dropped a few;
But not one Christmas Wish is lost,
Of all I bring to you.

Lucie Attwell. All of them introduced Teddy Bears into their scenes even if the Teddies were not always the key characters. Mabel Lucie Attwell, who was published by Valentines, achieved special success with her cards used at the start of the First World War. Throughout those years, people were kept in touch with scribbled, often heart-rending messages, echoed by the slogans and pictures on the cards: 'Jus' longin' to see you' with a winsome child peering through a gate.

In 1918, when postage for a card was doubled to one penny, the number of cards sent fell by about a half, although it was true that the need to send cards had also decreased. The war was over, and sending cards became more a holiday luxury or a birthday treat. A collection through the years would illustrate an interesting sequence of Teddy Bears and fashions. In the 1980s, one of the most popular series is of Teddy Edward, a little bear originally photographed by Patrick Matthews to illustrate stories his wife Mollie wrote in 1962 for *Watch with Mother* on British television. At about the same time a *Teddy Bear Comic* for children was produced, but it did not last long.

subjects for children, and specialist artists provided juvenile scenes as well: Florence Upton with her Golliwogs and dolls, Rose O'Neill with her kewpies, and, above all, the English Mabel

74

The Teddy, a favourite
companion in child portraiture,
shown here stealing the show in
two delightful pictures.

This fine array of Teddy
birthday cards features a gallery
of assorted Teddies.

To Wish my Dear Niece a Happy Birthday.

Blessings on you,
Niece of mine,
Fortune gifts and
favours shower,
Skies be blue,
a bright sun
shine,
Joy be with you
every hour.

A Joyous Birthday to You

Upon this little card I send
A little wish from a loving friend;
But may it bring you treasure bright,
And fill your Birthday with delight.

May fortune weave a golden thread Of joy and gladness round your head. May God protect you, dear, to-day & guide and guard your future way

Best Wishes for your Birthday.

A Glad and Happy Birthday.

A little card to wish you, dear,
A glad birthday and happy year.

77

This tuneful Teddy has a music box in his body which is operated by moving his head backwards and forwards. Today, sadly, the resulting melody is unrecognizable. Judging by the deeper colour at his joints, this bear was originally mauve. He was made in about 1925, possibly in France.

Musical Teddies

Besides the literature and art devoted to the Teddy Bear, the toy has even inspired music. In 1907 the American composer J.E. Bratton wrote a tune to honour Teddy and called it *Teddy Bears' Picnic* in celebration of the American President's bear-hunting exploits. The music would probably be forgotten now were it not for the famous lyrics, written by Jimmy Kennedy in England, which became a favourite children's song.

Henry Hall's band played *Teddy Bears' Picnic* with astonishing success in 1932, and it has remained a best-seller ever since, more recently being adopted as the theme song at meetings of Teddy Bear collectors.

THE LITTLE ORGAN GRINDER.

Teddy Bear Orchestra № 4. G. S.

"we are coming".
Teddy Bear Orchestra № 6. G.S.

Teddies march to the music of time on sheet music covers, including the world famous *Teddy Bears' Picnic*. On the early Teddy postcards also shown here Teddies make the music themselves.

Teddy Bears Today

Neither Bratton nor Kennedy would ever have imagined in their wildest dreams that one day real Teddy Bear Picnics would be held. On May 27, 1979 an enormous jamboree, at which 8000 guests were received, was sponsored in aid of Dr Barnado's Homes by no less a celebrity than the Marquess of Bath at his 'Stately Home' at Longleat. Bears were admitted free – of course –

although there was a charge for humans! The picnic was the work of the 'Good Bears of the World' movement, founded on October 27, 1970 (the birthday of Theodore Roosevelt) by James T. Ownley, the American Bearo Number One; the aim was to provide deprived children in hospitals with Teddies to cheer them up. At first, annual meetings of the movement were held in Berne, Switzerland, the Bear Town of the world, where bears have been kept since the Middle Ages.

The year 1983 was chosen as the 80th anniversary of Teddy's appearance and was celebrated with numerous Teddy events and by the issue of a number of commemorative bears. Steiff brought out images of the 'original' bear and bears dressed in a curious sort of trapper's hunting-gear, harking back to Roosevelt. Merrythought produced Edwardian Bears, Dean's provided Rockwell Bears, based on designs by Norman Rockwell, and in Britain Nisbet created an actual Teddy Roosevelt figure with his friend Teddy, while the German company of Hermann, founded in 1911, re-introduced Grandfather Bear. All were intended, of course, for collectors rather than

Opposite: 'Buzzy', a bear of rare
religious distinction and owner of a
wardrobe of birettas.

83

TUESDAY
This Little Bear Irons Clothes.

THUR
This Little Bea

MONDAY
This Little Bear Washes Clothes.

1906

WEDNESDAY
This Little Bear Mends Clothes.

Teddy Bears have much to teach us. Certainly, 'This Little Bear' (from the American 'Busy Bear' series of cards) appears to live an eminently virtuous life.

AY
akes Pies.

FRIDAY
This Little Bear Cleans House.

1910

SATURDAY
This Little Bear Goes to Market.

SUNDAY
This Little Bear Goes to Church.

January 1985 saw a Teddy Bears'
concert at the Barbican Centre in
London. The occasion attracted
numerous favourite occupants of
nurseries, bedrooms and attics.

children. At the same time, appropriately enough, *The Teddy Bear Magazine* for Arctophiles was launched. It is puzzling to know what the Greeks had to do with Teddy Bears – *arctos* is the ancient Greek word for bear – but this curious word has been adopted for bear-collectors.

The Teddy's 80th anniversary was also celebrated by a rally held at Philadelphia Zoo on June 25, 1983, that was even larger than the Longleat event. About 25,000 people attended the Philadelphia Teddy Bears' Picnic, among them the present managing director of the Steiff factory, accompanied by the first prototype bear

designed by Richard Steiff in 1902, insured for $40,000. (To emphasize its value, he had the bear chained to his waist.) The event was sponsored by various firms who share more than merely a goodwill interest in Teddies, among them toy-manufacturers, retailers, card-designers and publishers. Valuable prizes were offered for different classes of bear.

With this image of instant goodwill and his power to promote charitable causes, the idea has caught on, and Teddy Bears, and picnics for them, have become popular fund-raisers at local church fêtes and garden parties. Teddy owners are sometimes admitted for a reduced price, or alternatively a competition with different prize categories is staged: The Best Dressed Bear; the Prettiest; the Largest; the Smallest; and (difficult to determine) the Oldest. Only those who have been invited to judge an event of this kind will realize the tense feelings such a contest can arouse. A word of warning: each entrant *must* be very firmly labelled to prevent terrible mayhem at the end and cases of disputed ownership. Teddy Bear owners, it seems, are unwilling to admit that any other model was ever made in the same image. (But it was!)

No better example of the much-loved bear can be shown than this faithful friend made by the Merrythought Company. Despite his well-worn look and James Cagney expression, this is a bear of today, made only twenty years ago.

6.6.64.

"And turned to Archibald, my safe old bear
Whose woollen eyes looked sad or glad at me
Whose ample forehead I could wet with tears
Whose half-moon ears received my confidences
Who made me laugh, who never let me down.."

Dear Mr. Betjeman,

I should be very grateful if you would give me permission to quote the above lines from "Summoned by Bells" in a book which I am writing on toys.

I wanted to use it somewhat in the context of suggesting that whereas dolls were considered very much only the playthings of the female contingent, teddy bears and gollywogs were allowed in the nursery for small boys without any slur on their masculinity*In fact the modern psychologist would probably hint that here was the first tendency showing itself of the increasing importance of the role played by the father in modern marriage.

What I should really like of course is to wheedle out of you a photograph of Archibald for my book, but perhaps that asks too much, or you do not care for him to appear before the public eye...

In any case, I enclose an envelope in case you want to send a big haughty NO.

Yours sincerely,

Mary Hillier

Mrs. Mary Hillier.

So sorry. No teddington Jill + 40 Betters, London. by all means quote. Have no photograph of old Archie

* This would appear at the end of a chapter dealing with character dolls and toys that owed their invention to a literary image. I am sure you know that tradition has credited the first Teddy bear as being named after Theodore Roosevelt, who spared the life of a little bear cub when he was out hunting and Teddy Bear became finally Teddy Bear.

In looks better than old Archie

88

Archibald Ormsby-Gore, was the lifelong Teddy companion of the late Sir John Betjeman. Above: Archie with the young Betjeman. Left: Betjeman's own sketch of Archie on a letter to him from the author. Right: One of Phillida Gili's delightful illustrations of Archie in *Archie and the Strict Baptists* (1977).

The Appeal of the Teddy

What is the Teddy's special appeal that has made him survive as number one toy through wars and recessions? Questioned recently, some Teddy bear owners suggested that bears appealed because they 'looked' at you, while others thought that Teddies 'listened'. Psychologically, Teddies indicate the child's need for a secret confidant: an imaginary being, a Peter Pan shadow, a *Doppelgänger* vested in a favourite doll or toy animal, even in a live pet dog or cat; a surrogate little brother or sister who can be loved, trusted with one's most intimate thoughts, even, on occasion, abused without retaliation. It is the age-old German concept of the *Trösterlein*, the Little Comforter, which in earlier days had a religious significance. The late Sir John Betjeman, the Poet Laureate, whose own bear, Archibald Ormsby-Gore, was a treasured possession from early childhood, summed up the feeling in his autobiographical poem *Summoned by Bells*:

> And turned to Archibald, my safe old bear
> Whose woollen eyes looked sad or glad at me
> Whose ample forehead I could wet with tears
> Whose half moon ears received my confidence
> Who made me laugh, who never let me down.

In 1977 Sir John wrote a children's book about his bear, giving it the forbidding title *Archie and the Strict Baptists*. It was illustrated by Phillida Gili, the daughter of the engraver Reynolds Stone. The story is fun, and rather like the more recent hero Super Ted Archie makes himself brown-paper wings and *flies*.

Glimpses into the secret life of the
Teddy Bear. Left: A touching
example of Teddy affection. Below:
A special relationship.

TEDDY'S ROMANCE.

TWO HEARTS THAT BEAT AS ONE.

Archibald Ormsby-Gore went up to Oxford with Betjeman, and in the guise of Aloysius was immortalized in *Brideshead Revisited*, the novel written by Betjeman's contemporary Evelyn Waugh. The successful television serialization of *Brideshead Revisited* in 1983 was another reminder of the popularity of veteran Teddies. In the 1920s, Teddies were the hallmark of the effeminate aesthetes. In the 1980s, they have received the ultimate accolade. Examples of the pre-1914 bears are classed as *antiques*, and even veteran bears (those produced between the two world wars) are considered collectable. Sotheby's of London regularly includes bears in its auction sales. Occasionally the owner departs in tears, having left a childhood companion with a price on its head.

Not only old bears, but new ones as well are being collected, and clever novelties are constructed, not for children but especially for collectors. The late Peter Bull, who realized he had discovered a vast Underground Teddy Bear Movement, did a lot to promote the collecting craze, and a bear in his honour, Bully Bear, was produced by the House of Nisbet in Somerset. With an eye to future collecting, a delightful

90

Below: Bully Bear was produced in 1981 in honour of the late Peter Bull, the pioneer of Teddy Bear collecting. Bully has now made his way onto the printed page with great success.

Below: 'Little Tommy Tittlemouse' celebrates his 76th birthday at London's Bethnal Green Museum of Childhood. He still receives an annual birthday card from his original owner.

Right: Teddies now take their place among the cream of the world's art sold by the famous auctioneers Sotheby's. Here, rows of Teddies await the bids of rival would-be owners and a new life.

book by Pauline McMillan introduced the Zodiac Bears (a different character for each month), and their adventures in the village of Little Ticking. In fifty years time the book and the individual bears will be eagerly sought, and any of them would make a memorable gift for a special child.

Am I alone in finding a row of Teddy Bears set up for sale at auction a sad sight? They are like lost pets at the Battersea Dogs Home, but silent.

·THINKING·OF·YOU·

They are toys that have lost their children, toys that recall childhood past and finished. They are more nostalgic than dolls because they look so played with, a little worn or rubbed, a little soiled and still wearing some favourite jacket, scarf or brooch. They slump on the shelf or are handed to prospective buyers to be squeezed or prodded. They utter melancholy groans as they roll over, leaving a slight trickle of sawdust behind on the bench. Some folk care nothing for such treasures, others would not part with their old bear at any price. I do not know quite what to make of someone with a hundred Teddy Bears, since usually a bear is such a personal possession.

At Sotheby's in London there is steady, enthusiastic interest as the bears are held up. '£50?...£100?...£250'. Genuine early models in good condition fetch high prices, and just occasionally, for a unique type, the bidding goes even higher. What, dare one ask, would the price be for THE Pooh?

Perhaps I should leave the last word to a man who once owned this most famous bear of all, and all his life tried unsuccessfully to escape the character of 'Christopher Robin'. Mr Milne wrote in his autobiography, *The Enchanted Places*:

Every child has his Pooh, but one would think it odd if every man still kept his Pooh to remind him of his childhood. But my Pooh is different, you say. He is *the* Pooh. No, this only makes him different to you, not different to me. My toys were and are to me no more than yours were and are to you.

Teddy Bears' Picnic

Music: J. E. Bratton 1907   *Lyrics:* Jimmy Kennedy

If you go down in the woods today
You're sure of a big surprise
If you go down in the woods today
You'd better go in disguise.
For ev'ry Bear that ever there was
Will gather there for certain because,
Today's the day the Teddy Bears have their Picnic.

Ev'ry Teddy Bear who's been good
Is sure of a treat today
There's lots of marvellous things to eat,
And wonderful games to play
Beneath the trees where nobody sees
They'll hide and seek as long as they please,
Cos' that's the way the Teddy Bears have their Picnic.

If you go down in the woods today
You'd better not go alone
It's lovely down in the woods today
But safer to stay at home.
For ev'ry Bear that ever there was
Will gather there for certain, because
Today's the day the Teddy Bears have their Picnic.

"Do it now"

A Merry Christmas

TEDDY COOKS HIS XMAS DINNER.

Trio:
Picnic time for Teddy Bears,
The little Teddy Bears are having a lovely time today.
Watch them, catch them unawares
And see them picnic on their holiday.
See them gaily gad about,
They love to play and shout, They never have any cares;
At six o'clock their Mummies and Daddies
Will take them home to bed,
Because they're tired little Teddy Bears.

If you go down in the woods today
You'd better not go alone
It's lovely down in the woods today
But safer to stay at home.
For ev'ry Bear that ever there was
Will gather there for certain because
Today's the day the Teddy Bears have their Picnic.

GOODNIGHT EVERYBODY

Acknowledgements

The publishers gratefully acknowledge the kind help provided by the following, including those who supplied photographs, loaned items for photography and generally assisted with the making of this book:

BBC Hulton Picture Library 20; Fred Banbury and William Collins Sons & Co. Ltd/Random House N.Y. 57, 63 (Centre); Bethnal Green Museum of Childhood 91 (centre); M. Bird 58 (right); Peter Bull Estate/Enid Irving 91 (left); Matthew Corbett Ltd. 58 (left); Walt Disney Productions 54; J. Arthur Dixon Ltd 70 (left); EMI Music Publishing Ltd 80 (top left); Express Newspapers/Beaverbrook Newspapers Ltd 49, 50; Phillida Gili 89; Hawkley Studios Ltd 16; The Herbert Press, London/E.P. Dutton & Co. Inc. N.Y., *A Hug of Teddy Bears* by Peter Bull 88 (right); Ideal Toy Corporation 13; Denys Ingram Ltd 26, 29 (top), 32 (left); Library of Congress 15 (right); Lloyds Bank Ltd and Colin Anthony Richards, Executors of the Estate of E.H. Shepard and the E.H. Shepard Trust 51; Margarete Steiff Gmbh 17 (both); MPL Communications Ltd 49 (centre); John Murray (Publishers) Ltd 88 (right); Rose O'Neill and Henry McGrew Printing Inc. 74; W. Paxton 80; Keith Prowse & Co. Ltd 80; Raphael Tuck & Sons 1, 34 (right), 66, 90; R.W. Weekes Ltd, Tunbridge Wells 70 (right); E.H. Shepard, Copyright under the Berne Convention, USA Copyright E.P. Dutton & Co. Inc. 7, 52, 53, 63 (bottom), 92 (right), 93; Brian Sibley 41; Sotheby's 59; Windsor Spice, Reigate 43 (top & centre); Times Newspapers Ltd 70 (centre), 86, 91 (centre); The Washington Star 12 (left).

Particular thanks go to Jeremy Enness for photographing the selection of Teddy Bears from Joan Dunk's collection, pp. 6 (left), 8/9, 10, 19, 23, 24, 35, 55, 56, 61, 62, 64, 65 (right), 78, 82, 87, (© Black Pig Editions Ltd).

Every effort has been made to contact all the copyright holders of the images reproduced herein. Any queries should be addressed to:
Black Pig Editions Ltd, P.O. Box 99, Exeter, Devon, England.